Legendary Leadership Lessons

Raise the Bar & Then...

Legendary Leadership Lessons

Raise the Bar
& Then...

Author:
Nicholas I. Clement, Ed.D.
Ernest W. McFarland Citizen's Chair in Education
Northern Arizona University

Teachers
Change Brains
media

"*Dr. Nic Clement illustrates, in his endearing and humorous recollections of his own life experiences, that for leaders, there are leadership lessons to be found in even in daily situations. His passion for providing student and client centered leadership is evident, relatable, and thought provoking as he shares his expertise and experiences through storytelling. No matter where you are in your leadership career, this book will take you on your own journey through the leadership lessons that emerge day to day which can be immediately applied in your own school and leadership journey!*"

Courtney Cullum
Superintendent, Mazapan School
La Ceiba, Honduras

"*Dr. Clement's use of charming, whimsical tales challenges all of us to be honest with ourselves, laugh a bit and rally the kind of grit it takes to transport leadership to the next level.*"

Jill C. Louters
Superintendent, New Rockford-Sheyenne
School District
New Rockford-Sheyenne, North Dakota

Table of Contents

Introduction 17

Chapter One
Another Trip to the Dentist 21

Chapter Two
Raise the Bar & Then... 35

Chapter Three
Tale of Three Rodents 47

Chapter Four
Control Your Bullwinkle 63

Chapter Five
Free for All 73

Dedication

To my legendary family, wife Jolene, daughters Kerstin and Christina, son-in-law Tim and grandkids, Timmy and Kyle.
You never let me give up trying to find my swamp frog and encouraged me to share my stories.

Acknowledgment

Cirque du Soleil. One of the largest theatrical producers in the world and my go-to show in Las Vegas. I am fascinated watching the Cirque entertainers. People who have skills I could never dream to have, working together as a team on stage, creating mind numbing thrills.

If this book comes even close to Cirque like magic, it can be attributed to my team.

Judy Norstrant who created cover artwork that captured my big idea and a little of my childhood.

Pattie Copenhaver who formatted and designed the manuscript and brought life to the stories.

Jolene Clement who patiently read each draft and improved it with each suggestion.

Pat Buchanan who provided feedback at the early manuscript development phase.

Clark Clement who helped fill in the conceptual gaps.

Jennifer Anglin who did an amazing job editing the final draft.

Bethany Zito, Kriss Hagerl, Jill Louters, Courtney Cullum, and Dr. Jim Vaszauskas, busy educational leaders who took time to review the book.

Northern Arizona University College of Education who supports my work through the endowed Ernest W. McFarland Citizen's Chair in Education.

Tim Derrig, book agent extraordinaire, who supported and guided the project from a book title scrawled on a coffee shop napkin to finished manuscript.

A special tribute to Janet Herman for editing our first book and for her devotion to the Flowing Wells School District.

Introduction

Groucho Marx was a comic genius. Film actor and comedian, Groucho, also hosted a T.V. game show called *You Bet Your Life*. During the show, if the contestant said the "secret word," a duck would come down with a hundred dollars in winning cash.

Unlike Groucho, I won't keep you guessing. The secret word for this book is "engagement." My goal is that the text will challenge you to question, think, and ultimately improve your leadership skills.

If you find yourself fact checking, mentally fist pumping, and yelling some fourth grade words loud enough that I can hear, you win the cash.

Leaders always win when staff, students, and customers engage.

Sweet Tweets

As you read this book, I know you will have the urge to tweet the leadership lessons to your colleagues and friends. I also know your time is valuable as you squeeze out time to read on a plane, over morning coffee, or waiting for your new tires to be balanced. This may be the first book ever with embedded tweets designed for your fast paced, multi-tasking, reading e-mails in the elevator life.
Just not while you drive—Mr. Serrell.

Chapter One

Another trip to the Dentist

Chapter One

Another trip to the Dentist

If you read my previous book, this chapter title alone triggers some thoughts and possibly a fear chill. First, a promise was made not to have readers suffer through another dental story. Second, sequels usually turn high hopes into hopelessness. Anyone who bought popcorn, Jujyfruits and a ticket to *Godfather II, Grease 2* or *Revenge of the Sith* can relate. Hold your twitter feed, I know *Revenge of the Sith* was technically a prequel.

Leadership is all about risk and reward. Risking another dental story lesson hoping it will reward you with more than the Dum Dum sucker I got from the dentist after my visit when I was little. Root beer was my favorite and I would rummage the bowl until I found one. This is not a book about the many illogical aspects of growing up, but getting a sugary root beer sucker for not screaming after having a cavity filled which was caused by sugary suckers is one of them. Liver and lima beans are another childhood conundrum I will never understand, but will always have the gag reflex associated with this monthly supper ritual. Even the family dog turned down this culinary combination.

Rounding out the top three "what were my parents thinking" hit parade was the safety rope. Safety rope makes perfect sense for rock climbing, swift water rescue, and parasailing. Safety rope becomes an oxymoron when your mom and dad tie you to your two brothers and then allow you to join them swimming in Lake Michigan during hurricane-like conditions. They had great intentions. They were concerned about the undertow created by the ten foot waves. Solution, tie the boys together so if the youngest (me) gets swept out to sea, I would be saved by the rope attached to my oldest brother. (I know Lake Michigan is a freshwater lake. *Swept out beyond the sandbar of a freshwater lake created by glaciers* just doesn't have the same literary drama.)

Side note: *This book may be my last chance for a Pulitzer, so please cut me some slack and save your Amazon and Yelp critical reviews for the next leadership book you read. There are three sure things in life; death, taxes and a new book on leadership.*

My mom and dad's plan had a "parents of the year" trophy waiting to be awarded except for one knotty flaw. What if the undertow decided to take my oldest brother first? I know, he was smarter, stronger, better looking, didn't have to go to the dentist as often, and got his driver's license on the first try, but stranger things have happened. Like my mom rescuing three baby raccoons and thinking that we could raise and train them to be loving pets. After a year, the only loving thing about the raccoons was the trip we took to drop them off at the Kalamazoo Milham Park Zoo.

Four paragraphs in and I already have a leadership lesson to preach— my mom would be proud. Effective leaders cannot rely on the strongest to become a rescue anchor for other team members. Undertow hits organizations often times without warning with "older, stronger, smarter" employees leaving for various reasons. Effective leaders create organizational culture and climate that values and embeds professional development, making everyone a strong and effective swimmer. Have a succession plan in every leadership position in your organization. Don't tie your team together with a rope; tie your team together with training and experience.

Succession planning— the tie that binds

I know it is early to create tension through incongruence. A Safety Rope Leadership Lesson does not appear to remotely align with my chapter title. I understand the stress this causes with many readers. Heck, (wanted to use another word I learned in fourth grade, but grandma

Elma would not approve) I am stressed out and I am the author and on blood pressure meds. I have a solution. Consider the safety rope story and lesson a good prequel, like the movie *Batman Begins*.

Side note: During my career as a Superintendent, my favorite analogy to an event or task that I despised doing was having a root canal. For example, I would rather have a root canal than travel two hours to the state capital to meet and lobby legislators for adequate school funding.

My intent is not to generalize and characterize all legislators with this analogy, just the ones who gave no eye contact or worse, gave me the "stop whining, when I was a kid we were lucky to have chalk," stare eye.

I would rather have a root canal than attend a party where I am always cornered by the self-proclaimed smartest person in the room whose solution is to "just run schools like a ." It has always fascinated me that some people, including my favorite state legislators who are not trained educators, think they earned a teaching college degree at the same time they received their high school diploma. Thirteen years of going to school makes them an expert in education. Using that same logic, my hundreds of hours as a dental patient should enable me to put "D.D.S." behind my name. Believe me, you don't want me anywhere close to your mouth with a sharp object in my hand.

Recently, I added to my patient hours, undergoing an emergency root canal. Based on this experience, I can no longer with good conscious ever link a root canal procedure with things I loathe. In fact, I was so impressed with the diagnosis and treatment performed by my endodontist with support from my family dentist, I will use root canal as an analogy for an effective leadership vision. I will resolve my cognitive dissonance by drilling down on the lessons I learned in three areas critical to keeping organizations and teeth healthy: creating a client centered culture and cutting edge tools and technology.

A brief back story is necessary to fully appreciate and understand how a root canal can be connected to leading continuous organizational improvement.

Raise the Bar & Then...

It's Thanksgiving weekend and I am enjoying playing games at the park with the grandkids. We had all recovered from spending the previous summer together.

At the end of summer, I knew it was time for them to go back to school and me to find some work when we were playing shark attack in the pool. I stood up and started lecturing Kyle and Timmy about shark attack rules. I told them if they were going to play with grandpa, they were going to adhere to my rules. At that moment, I froze and mentally took this picture, a 63 year old grandpa, standing up in the shallow end, lecturing about shark attack rules to his 6 and 9 year old grandkids like they were in a graduate class. That was a sure sign that they needed a break from grandpa.

As I began to give my granddaughter an underdog on the swing (not sure where "underdog" originated, but if I start going down that rabbit hole, I am afraid we won't come back and even Alice came back), I felt a severe pulsating ache in my lower back molar. Although it subsided, the pain returned and continued throughout the night.

Saturday morning and instead of playing kickball (another mystery unwritten rules universally embraced), I am in the fetal position in a chair. Incredible how a one inch tooth can dominate and make your entire life and body miserable when it starts to go bad. I know you are dying for a leadership lesson here. Whatever one I give, my sense is (I am a university professor and we are the only profession allowed to start sentences with "my sense is") that you will find my lesson inadequate. Let's cut out the middle man and you go right for it, create your own bad tooth leadership metaphor and email me. I will pick one and include it in the 2nd edition and give you an author credit. Only one catch, we need to sell enough of the 1st edition to reprint. Yes, I am a marketing genius.

After quickly tiring of the moans and self-pity (not sure which was louder), my wife declared that she was going to try and call a dentist to get me in on an emergency basis. I woefully mumbled the odds of finding a dentist to see me on a holiday weekend were about the same as winning the lottery. We bought a ticket that night! Dr. Joseph

Larsen answered his phone and indicated that he was at his office doing paperwork and his daughter and a friend were helping clean his office to make some money to help pay for a school trip. He said he would see me immediately.

When I arrived, we both were dressed for Saturday morning in the desert (flip flops, shorts, and a baseball cap). One big difference, Dr. Larsen's shirt was clean and didn't have drool stains. He apologized for his appearance. I apologized for interrupting his holiday weekend. At this point, Dr. Larsen's appearance was the last thing on my mind. I saw no connection between his dental skills and knowledge with his Hawaiian shirt, but he did. He quickly stepped into a room and put on his white coat. Quick leadership lesson: appearance matters.

Although it was a challenge without his assistant, Dr. Larsen proceeded to conduct a full exam including x-rays. He indicated that my problem could be complex and might require a root canal. He provided some meds for pain relief and made an appointment to see me first thing on Monday.

He warned me about the Vicodin side effects, explaining that although he would write a prescription, I should stick with ibuprofen and use it only as a last resort. Saturday night, molar is playing ragtime extra loud on the pain player piano. I thought it was Vicodin time. After two hours, I was seriously questioning my decision making, not only at that moment, but during my entire career.

Three hours have passed, now laid out on the hallway floor like I was taking a nap in kindergarten, clutching my smart phone (I have joined the digital generation—even in my darkest hour, got to have a phone in hand), scrolling through the Web MD Vicodin side effects mentally checking off every effect I was experiencing. Dizziness. Check. Nausea. Check. Headache. Check. Check. Check. Check. I got 100% so far! Vomiting; quick scamper to the porcelain altar to earn extra credit. As I found my new resting place on the bathroom shower mat, I was wondering about another life mystery: what part of this

Vicodin experience could be close to addictive? Through the next day I continued to score high on my SAT (Side Affects Test..add it to the list, I know you are keeping one...he should have used "effect"...SET not as clever...I choose clever over correct word choice). I had never been so happy to see a dentist on a Monday morning as when I walked through Dr. Larsen's office door.

Leadership lesson: "last resort" is an idiom, you idiot (me the author, not you the reader). It doesn't mean the last resort has ocean views but not turn down service and a water slide. "Last resort" means all viable options have been exhausted, and there's an understanding that this option has known and unknown side effects. Leaders need to be patient, cautious, pragmatic, and have clear future foreseeability before making a "last resort" type decision.

Don't take Vicodin when Tylenol will do

No shorts, flip flops or hats today. Dr. Larsen's assistants were all dressed for success and acted the same. I was welcomed with a smile and treated with kindness first, registration and insurance card later.

The time between getting settled in the dental chair and Dr. Larsen walking in the room was seconds, not minutes. I didn't even have time to fix and adjust a pressure bottle that I hit with my leg as I was climbing in the chair. Immediately, it starting hissing and his dental assistant who followed me in but didn't observe my klutzy move, tried to fix it. Dental offices are stressful enough for me when it comes to following directions. Sit in the right chair, open my mouth wide enough, bite down on the cotton hard enough, and don't gag and accidentally bite the dental assistant. Now, look what I have done, broken what I imagine is a very expensive piece of equipment, and there is no way my co-pay will cover it. Usually I don't give myself up so quickly. Blame it on Vicodin residual effects or, more likely, my new first rule: don't lie and irritate a dentist right before he begins to fire up the drill. As I was confessing my sin, Dr. Larsen and his assistant were working to get the container sealed. Three tries and the hissing ceased.

After additional tests, Dr. Larsen determined I needed an immediate root canal. He indicated that he did not have time to do the root canal due to other scheduled patients and proceeded to have his staff begin calling multiple endodontists to see if they could get me an appointment. I was thinking, I already won the lottery once, the chances of getting an appointment with a root canal specialist today would be way beyond the lottery odds, more like the legislature fully funding school odds. Wish I was back in the Superintendency because next year schools are getting a raise. Dr. Larsen's assistant was able to get me an appointment with Dr. Paul Hobeich, a root canal specialist, in 20 minutes. Dr. Larsen said to leave now and his staff indicated that they would take care of all the paperwork later. An assistant guided me out, down the hall to the left then right, and left. How did she know I suffer from MOCS (medical office confusion syndrome—a condition in which you are unable to navigate from the exam room to the reception area)?

Quick drive, usual unparalleled parking, and I burst into Dr. Hobeich's office, thinking, right, 20 minutes really means one hour after I have to write my life history and get my banker to vouch for my marginal credit standing. No clipboard, no inkless pen, not even time to look at last year's People magazine. The receptionist gently greeted me with "We are expecting you. Let me take you to Dr. Hobeich's examination room. We will take good care of you." Now I was gasping for breath, not from the rush between dental offices, but from the "be our guest, be our guest" approach from the entire office staff.

Like Dr. Larsen's exam room, I hardly had the drool bib clipped and Dr. Hobeich arrived with a cheerful yet, "let's not do a lot of small talk because you are in pain" hello. I am sure he was grateful that I didn't kick and damage a piece of his equipment in saddling up. No offense Dr. Larsen, Dr. Hobeich's equipment was more expensive. I am sure he was given a heads up through a warning posted on the least wanted dental patient Facebook page.

Dr. Hobeich began my treatment with a clear description of the root canal procedure from beginning to end along with alerting me to a potential problem which could not be detected with the x-ray (cracked tooth below the gum line). Leadership lesson alert: Leaders anticipate problems they cannot see and plan solutions which they hope won't be needed.

Less than an hour later, I walked out of Dr. Hobeich's office with no pain and lots of gain. Three hours later I received a call from Dr. Larsen, yes, Dr. Larsen, not a high-pitched computer-synthesized "hello....we are pretending to care about your care by having a machine contact you...and the IRS is going to sue you" Dr. Larsen was following up to make sure I was O.K. and to help me make the follow-up crown appointment.

The leadership lesson is that leaders must strive to create a similar client-centered culture like I encountered during my root canal experience. Client-centered culture requires more than a focus on improving customer service. It requires a mindset that our clients are the center of the school universe and a collective action plan to meet their immediate and long term needs. Little details make a big difference.

Little details =
Big difference

Dr. Larsen's and Dr. Hobeich's offices looked nothing like my first visit to a dentist. I still remember the funky burnt smell of my tooth being drilled on by a device with so many pulleys and gears that it qualified as a Rube Goldberg cartoon. Although the smoke was fun to watch coming out of my mouth, the enamel shrapnel going up my nose and into my eyes put a damper on the thrill.

As I had waited for Dr. Larsen to fix the pressure container, I had asked about some of the new technology that I hadn't broken. Digital radiography, intraoral cameras, curing lights, state of the art composites, high speed drills, lasers, and new desensitizers. He would have continued, but the hiss was fixed and he focused on doing the same to my molar.

Couldn't have same discussion with Dr. Hobeich. Had gotten numbed up so fast that I couldn't ask any questions. Dr. Hobeich added an extra precaution to keep me from distracting his focus—he stretched a thin rubber barrier across my mouth exposing only the problem tooth. Leaders should learn from this technique—pinpoint problems, conceal distractions, solve the problem. I need to add a step, thanks to Dr. Hobeich: pinpoint and magnify the problem. Dr. Hobeich did not rely on his "naked eye" vision. He rolled out a ginormous microscope to help guide his hands as he extracted the delicate nerves and then inserted with precision, replacement posts. When's the last time you read a book that used *ginormous* as an adjective? Know what you are thinking, and I agree, I am kind of a big deal when it comes to leadership genre authors.

Leaders should not rely on their naked eye when visioning. Build your own ginormous microscope through experience, education, and teamwork.

Besides being schooled in modern dentistry, my walk-away lesson was that although schools have made progress in technology, leaders must continue to step up and create classrooms with cutting edge technology and the tools needed to promote high level learning. Unfortunately, too many of today's classrooms look and smell like my 1960's dental office. Generation Z demands and is reliant on technology. Leaders need to exceed that demand.

First chapter recap, or now that I think I am a semi-expert in modern dentistry, first chapter milled crown (crown that can be digitally constructed in the dentist office, same day; no temp cap needed).

After a nerve-jumping start reliving some random childhood traumas, I settled down, and transformed excruciating tooth pain into a leadership lesson excursion. Watch for my newest bumper sticker: "If you can lead, thank a dentist."

Reprinted with permission from the May 2017 issue of School Administrator magazine, published by AASA, The School Superintendents Association.

Chapter 1 Engagers

- What is the succession plan for your organization?

- Share your own bad tooth leadership lesson metaphor.

- Describe three practices you would implement or change to create a stronger client centered culture.

- Identify the "slow drill" technologies in your organization and the steps you are taking to lead your organization through the digital transformation.

Chapter Two

Raise the Bar & Then...

Chapter Two

Raise the Bar & Then...

Think we need to pause at this point and clarify a perception you may be forming. I do have mom and dad issues. Not the "put a psychotherapist's kid through college" personal demons, although the red boot line up after recess might have been worth a session or two. My parent issues deal with the truth that they exceeded the saying, "your parents get wiser every year you get older." When I was young, I rarely won an argument with my mom, and now I am taking her side.

In retrospect, my parents were progressive visionaries. February 1972, senior year, my mom and dad have a rare two-on-one conversation with me. We didn't even have "the talk" this way. For that I was given a pamphlet and at the same time was told I needed to get those magazines under my bed thrown away.

Our conversation went like this: "Hey Nic, spring break is coming up. Why don't you go down to Florida and visit your brothers. Take an extra week off from school and combine it with spring break. Ask a couple of friends if they want to go with you and take the station wagon." Go to Florida, on my own, with two friends, skip school, take the car (you are thinking it would have been even cooler if they let me take the other car, but it was also a station wagon), and hang out with my older brothers. I need to update Wikipedia, and give my parents credit for inventing "Road Trip."

The same parents who had to take out a second mortgage to replace the fence I plowed into during Driver's Ed are packing my bags for Florida. Sensing a rare opening in a window that hadn't been open since 1966 when my parents let me take the trolley to Fisherman's Wharf in San Francisco, alone, I went for it and asked if I could skip the senior prom. Quick "NO" response in a "you are really pushing your luck, son" tone.

Raise the Bar & Then...

My mom had this rule, unwritten like all the rules, that we had to go to both our junior and senior prom. At the time, controlling; looking back, visionary. If rules are unwritten, no need to get an eraser to change, giving us kids less time to formulate our argument. My mom wanted to have a full set of pictures to hang in the hallway for her grandkids to laugh at and make fun of Dad's gold paisley tuxedo.

After making sure they weren't suffering from a high fever delirium, I jumped into action. Best friends Terry and Dean were in, answer was yes before I even got to the part about taking the station wagon.

First step, follow the rules and fill out the family trip request ...to get the five days excused by the school administration and teachers. I was visiting my brothers, Terry was going to visit his grandparents on the Gulf Coast. We thought we had the family angle covered.

Papers signed, 1972 style social media alerted (squeaked it out in all caps on a few classroom chalkboards), and we were on the road in the dark green Mercury station wagon, sitting in the front two rows with that evil back facing third seat flattened. Not for luggage. I am not sure we brought any. It was more of a coming of age statement. All three of us had spent many hours sitting in that seat on family trips.

Travel plans reflected our age when we were developing our strategic short term and long term goals. Threw that line in to give this story some relevance to leadership. Actually, we had no plans and if I told you our goals, I would be fracturing my tale.

The trip through Indiana was uneventful until we reached I-465, the beltway by-pass for Indianapolis. No disrespect to Indiana, but not the most exciting state to drive through. We were curious and interested in a side trip to a town on the map called French Lick. Like Mom's, our trip rules were unwritten and like kick-ball, universally adopted. No side trips. No stops period, except in an emergency. Going to the bathroom and eating did not fit our definition of emergency. Getting gas was it. We adjusted quickly to getting our bathroom business done before the pump stopped. We were thankful for the 1970s pumps that would ding after every gallon.

There are some real advantages to youth. A 600 mile bathroom interval was no problem. If I recall, we had a contest to see who could hold it the longest. Not only on this trip but all four years of high school. Now, I include a bathroom stop when I go two blocks to grocery shop, or the five trips to Home Depot to pick up the right size screw.

Even more depressing, while going through security this morning for the flight I am writing this chapter on, the agent asked if I was 75 or older. He wanted to let me through the old person scanner where I didn't have to take off my shoes. I was on the third day with the same socks, pre-crust state, so I said yes. I did get a pat down after going through screening. I told the frisking agent that his colleague thought I looked 75 and asked if my abs felt like a 75 year old. Got the "get your belt, shoes, wallet, laptop, keys, and four ounces of youth cream and get to your gate before I call a supervisor" scowl.

Followed orders with two bathroom stops before boarding. Two hours into this trip and I need to go again, but haven't figured out how to time the unbuckle, jump, aisle run and not violate the no standing in line airplane rule. Also have a fear of blue water. Will tap my inner road trip youth and hold it until we land in Grand Rapids.

Back to the 1972 spring road trip. Remember the exit off of the I-465 bypass? We didn't. We had to travel an extra hour circling Indianapolis. Taking the I-65 exit, was the only advice my mom gave me along with don't drink, smoke, do drugs, or get arrested, and don't lie in the sun too long on the beach.

> *Don't drink, smoke,*
> *do drugs, or lie on the*
> *beach too long—Mom*

Broke our rule. Had to stop and eat at the original Kentucky Fried Chicken restaurant. Back on the road and Dean was driving in the rain, hit a slick spot, and the station wagon does a 360. Dean's expert driving skills got us back on the road without hitting a fence or rolling down a hill towards a river. I know what your thinking, lucky we switched drivers after I finished that last original recipe wing. Correction, wasn't called original recipe; extra crispy wasn't introduced until 1974. Go ahead, grab that phone, fact check me. It will also calm your shakes. Been about 10-15 minutes since you searched French Lick.

Georgia state line and Terry's turn to drive. The green Mercury wagon was becoming hipper with every mile. Function trumped form as Dean and I stretched out for a short nap. 200 miles later we were tossed awake to find Terry swerving the car down I-75 as we crossed the Florida border at 1 a.m. Before we could grab the wheel, Terry yelled with excitement, "Isn't this great, they have little lights on the road and it's just like a slalom ski course!" At that moment, Dean and I were rethinking our no stop rule.

Disney World. 4 a.m. We are the first and only car in line at the gate. leadership lesson time? There is a myth in leadership lore that effective leaders are the first to turn the lights on and last to flip the off switch. Will disprove this hypothesis (again, let me remind the readers, I am a university professor) when you join us after we get a few hours of sleep under the stars and the Disney World "Where Dreams Come True" sign.

We were still first to drive in and follow the friendly parking cast members' directions, guiding the Mercury into Goofy 4. Then it happened, we were no longer first in line at the ticket counter. Thousands of people suddenly appeared and they were all ahead of us. Not sure this was the Magical World of Disney we had dancing in our heads as we were navigating the Smokey Mountains in Tennessee.

In addition to the fact that roads in Florida were built with reflectors to help keep older drivers in their lane, and Michigan roads were built for snow plowing, we didn't take into account a few other factors as our trip progressed.

Disney World had only been open for less than a year. It was spring break. It was a beautiful day. We attended a small school where the wait at lunch between the first student in line and the last was about two minutes.

As we wandered with wonder, we wondered if we would do more than wander. Lines everywhere. Long, long, long lines. Our dream of returning to Gobles High School as legends and having our trip pics in a special yearbook section were about to be shattered. We needed to find a ride and find one fast.

A pink building, lots of flags, small boats entering a tunnel and no lines! We ran through the railing maze, got our directions from Mickey, climbed in, boats gently bumping into each other as they entered the mysterious dark passageway. The dream is still alive.

As our eyes dilated, our ears are greeted with song. A song we had never heard before, but by the end of the ride, we would never forget. The lyric was simple, catchy and even though Terry and I had been kicked out of church choir once, we found ourselves singing along. As the boats moved along, we did notice that the song only had one verse which was repeated over and over. Our kind of song.

Darkness turned into a full light show spotlighting dolls representing different countries. The dolls were moving their arms, heads, and bodies in sync with the music. Our 18 year old dim light bulbs finally turned on; the song "It's a Small World After All" gave a message of how we are all connected throughout the world.

It wasn't the Matterhorn, but if social media were around, our selfies would have been impressive. The boats reached Denmark, and they bumped into each other. Normal boat behavior. Boats were not moving after the bump. Abby normal boat behavior (apologies to Mel Brooks, *Young Frankenstein* is my all-time favorite movie and I have been waiting all my life to drop a reference). Boats are dead in the water yet the music and doll clacking was very much alive and well, one hour alive and well.

During all 500 "It's a small world" verses, not one passenger moved, no Disney rage, Mickey said keep our hands and feet in the boat at all times and no one wanted to disappoint Mickey. Leadership lesson: environment and culture influence behavior.

Attack the senses— change behavior

We had the opportunity to break the rules. The water was only two feet deep and there were walk areas on each side of the boat. We calmly remained in our seats because Disney had created the Happiest Place on Earth through environmental design and universally understood values. Like Disney nation, leaders must continually improve the customer experience through attacking our senses and immersing us in non-negotiable organizational principles and values.

The boats started move. No spontaneous applause as if, even that gesture, would offend the mouse. Daylight began to breakthrough and an aura was created by either our pupils adjusting or Snow White, who greeted us at the end of the ride. As we stepped off, she smiled and softly tweeted, "On behalf of Walt, we are sorry about the ride breaking down. Here is a free E Ticket for you to enjoy another ride."

If you were born before 1970, skip this next section where I explain the Disney E-Ticket. If you were born after 2000, you are critiquing me for misusing the verb *tweeted*.

Up until 1982, you purchased a Disney ticket pack which included a certain number of A, B, C, D and very few E tickets. To give some perspective, the Teacup ride was an A ticket and the Matterhorn roller coaster was an E ticket.

I don't recall if we used our E-Ticket, but I will never forget the "It's a Small World" song and Snow White coming to the rescue. Leaders make mistakes. Organizations make mistakes. Legendary leaders figure out ways to come to the rescue and turn the mistake into an E Ticket.

Turn errors into E-tickets

The rest of our two week spring break adventure included both highlights and lowlights. Highlight: Terry's grandparents' retirement village on the Gulf Coast unofficially made us honorary members and we were treated like royalty. Learned and got addicted to shuffleboard.

Lowlight: having a semi-truck merge into the green Mercury's side. Again, function over form. Although the phone booth call from a busy Orlando intersection to dad was difficult, the wagon was drivable and we went on our way.

We returned home to a heroes' welcome except for one minor detail. Someone reported to the principal that we did not have our family with us the entire trip. First day back included a trip to the principal's office. Our five days of excused absences became five days of unexcused absences with all the penalties. Consequences were firm, fair, and forgettable. My senior year Florida journey with Terry and Dean was life-changing.

One minor regret. I did miss a track meet. I think the team actually scored higher at that meet because I wasn't a great track star. I had some great aspirations. In 7th grade I thought I was going to be the next Dick Fosberry. My dad helped me build a sawdust high jump pit next to the raccoon cage. They weren't the most encouraging bleacher fans as I practiced the techniques Coach Serrell taught me.

Although I finally agreed with the raccoons and gave up on my high jump career, Coach Serrell never gave up. If I cleared a height, he was first to celebrate. He would raise the bar and not walk away. He stayed, watched me try the new height, and after I knocked the bar off, provided me immediate, non-judgmental, specific feedback. I know now, that at the time, he knew that I wasn't going to break any high jump records or even place in a meet. That didn't matter to Coach. What mattered was I was interested and motivated to try. What mattered was forming good technique and habits at the beginning. Coach Serrell lived his teaching and coaching by the credo "you rarely break bad habits and always improve good habits."

Leadership lesson quiz time (my clever way to connect these two—wait for it—totally unrelated stories). How is an unauthorized senior trip to Florida like high jumping? Asking the reader? Are you having a cold sweat flashback to sitting for the Miller Analogies Test when you were trying to get into grad school?

High jumper : Bar : Leader : (a. profit, b. influence, c. title, d. retirement)

My mom and dad seemed to raise the bar and never walk away. A simple leaf notebook for 9th grade science wasn't high enough. My mom thought it would be more challenging to seal each leaf and the written description in clear paper used to line cabinets and then cut around each leaf. As usual, she over supervised my scissor work, making sure I used my non-dominate right hand. My teacher, Mr. Davis, gave my mom an A for creativity and me a B- because I included a poison ivy leaf in the oak family section. Upside, leaf notebook will look like new when displayed at my funeral.

Then a miracle occurred, my parents walked away from the high jump pit and let me work on clearing the highest height ever—coping with real life. During the Florida trip, every decision was mine to make, every problem, mine to solve and all the consequences were mine to own.

Legendary leaders practice what I learned from mom, dad and Coach Serrell, they constantly raise the bar and then know when to stay close and when to walk away.

Chapter 2 Engagers

- Tell a "Snow White to the Rescue" story which recently occurred to you.

- Relate a leadership scenario where you "raised the bar" and should have walked away, and one where you should have stayed.

Chapter Three

Tale of Three Rodents

Chapter Three

Tale of Three Rodents

High school, junior year. Favorite cold January night activity: varsity basketball practice. Favorite end of practice tradition: one-on-one full court. Coach would put a basketball in the center, number us off one through five then line us up on opposite sides. Coach would call number "2," and if you were a 2, you would race out to get first possession, and then it was full court one-on-one. Coach knew what he was doing, making us dig deep when we were already exhausted from a full practice.

Made a shot, a left-handed hook—NBA worthy move. While making my defensive sprint down the court, felt and heard something pop in my left leg. I immediately begin to limp and hop on my good leg. I could describe it like when a thoroughbred racehorse pulls up. As much as I value metaphors as a literary device, I really didn't share any athletic attributes with a thoroughbred racehorse when I was in high school and I certainly don't now.

After practice, I tried out the new training room Jacuzzi. Warmed me up for my mile walk home (in the snow), but did little to alleviate the hurt and hobble. Getting ready for school the next day, and I couldn't get my jeans over my left calf. Did I mention the pain? Good thing Vicodin wasn't on the market yet (save your data, Vicodin was first introduced in 1978).

Mom had left for her nursing job in Battle Creek, and dad was downstairs cooking our favorite breakfast, smoked link sausages, the little ones, and dollar sized pancakes. Later in life when I brought back my family to visit in the summer, my dad would start cooking this breakfast early, and as the grandkids came downstairs, they were awakened by the same glorious smell. During the summer, dad added fresh blueberries to the pancakes, lots of fresh blueberries from the Fritz's farm.

Dad had some first-hand experience with medical issues, having had a double bypass. No time for a pig in a blanket, we were off to the emergency room at Bronson Hospital in Kalamazoo. Doc took one look and ordered a gurney and rushed me to a hospital room. I had suffered a severe muscle tear, causing internal bleeding. At the time, the treatment was to keep the leg elevated, immobile, and be confined to a hospital bed for about 4 days. The weather was bad that week, so it kept my throngs of get well-wishers away from visiting me (at least that's what my parents told me).

One nurse who had just recently graduated from Western Michigan University, sensed my anxiety and on the second day, asked if I had slept OK. I did mention that the groans from the other rooms were a little louder than the night before. She indicated that my next door neighbor died last night, and the multiple code blues might have created some extra commotion. Now, that news totally reduced my stress and took my mind off the absence of cards, flowers, and visitors surrounding
my bed.

As I was sucking down my last green Jello square, she gently suggested I replace my self-pity with a book. She asked about my favorite subject. We then had a brief conversation about the new Introduction to Psychology class I was taking at Gobles High School, brief because another code blue was going off down the hall.

The next day, she dropped off her freshman Psychology text. I was getting bored and a little motion sick from using the remote to raise and lower the bed, and even the ladies who worked the volunteer auxiliary skipped my room, so I started reading. I didn't look up from the Psychology text until supper (dinner if you grew up west of the Mississippi). Liver, lima beans and milk with a bendy straw. Obviously my mom had stopped by the hospital food service department on her way to work that morning. Suddenly I had a better understanding of the negative reinforcement chapter. Kept reading and they removed the adverse stimulus.

I recovered from my injury, recovered from the humiliating wheelchair ride to the car without even a balloon in my hand, yet never recovered from the nurse's gift. The more I read about B.F. Skinner and Sigmund Freud, the more I wanted to read.

A year later and time to register for freshman elective classes at the University of Michigan. No brainer, Psychology 101. Wondering why only one elective? Did so spectacularly on the entrance exams, that I was required to take an Evelyn Wood Speed Reading class, a developmental writing class, and Economics 90. I will answer the questions you are thinking out loud. I passed my writing class with flying colors, although the flag was at half-mast. Got a D in Economics. Met with the Econ teacher after grades were posted and argued every final exam essay and received no additional points. Walking out of his office and calculating what a four credit D would do to my already code blue grade point average, I did a quick add of the points for each question. I may have needed Econ 90, but the University Professor needed Math 95. He had added wrong. Never so happy to get a C in my life.

Add twice; grade once

I dreaded my walk off campus twice a week to the little house where I took speed reading. Slow walk to speed read. In contrast, I was psyched to attend my freshman Psychology 101 class held at Markley Hall.

Class scope gave equal time to Sigmund Freud and B.F. Skinner, starting with Dr. Freud. I found his dream theories fascinating, and I did my first paper based on a study I conducted, interviewing elementary students regarding their dreams. My hypothesis was that based on Freud's theory that dreams represent our inner wishes, we can remember more of our dreams at a younger age when our superego is less developed and less apt to censor with disconnected imagery.

I contacted the elementary principal in my home town, and asked if I could interview some elementary students about their dreams and he said no problem. Will give you a moment to adjust your jaw because it just dropped. Naïve first year college student meets the naïve first year principal equals research ethics train wreck.

As I was transcribing my last interview tape, using the Dictaphone borrowed from my dad, listening to a first grader talk about his dream when he was flying with the birds to get away from their cat, the dorm room phone rang. Dorm Rooms at Alice Lloyd Hall had just been upgraded so you didn't have to go down the hall to use the pay phone. Still had to go down to use the community bathrooms. Our hall had converted our bathroom to coed except on parent weekends. Reminder: it was the 70's, and the University of Michigan. Won't try and explain it because I still don't really understand it. Goes in the "what were we thinking" column.

My dad was on the phone. Thinking this must be important because we didn't phone, write letters or come home from college on weekends, but we were a close family. Dad, who at the time was the school district attorney, said I needed to erase those dream interview tapes immediately and destroy any notes taken during my study. Didn't have the courage to tell him I had already turned in the paper. Erased the tape, got my A, and if I interviewed you for the study, you would be about 55 years old. I apologize for any trauma it caused in your life, but the statue of limitations has expired.

In the next chapter we studied B.F. Skinner, the father of behaviorism. This unit included a lab experiment assignment. Exciting moment for me; got to wear a white coat, work in an animal lab which wasn't outside, and the lab didn't include raccoons giving me their little middle finger when I got close.

First day and we were given a Plexiglas box, a metal bar on the front side with wires attached to a dispenser with a chute leading to a small trough below the bar. There was also a button remote attached with a cord to the dispenser. Aha, I can now trace and explain my current TV remote addiction, the hospital bed, and psychology lab. Freud is a genius.

In a previous class, we had studied this device named after its inventor, the Skinner Box. We were also introduced to our experimental subject, a white rat with peerie marble-like pink eyes. I immediately named mine Ralph. Ralph the Rat. Ralph was before his time when it came to his home. He lived in a shiny metal container high rise.

The lab instructor demonstrated how to slide Ralph's home out and then carefully pick him up and place him in the Skinner Box. We were also instructed in other lab animal care procedures and routines, including the regular feeding and watering schedule.

The lab was designed to test Skinner's theory of positive reinforcement. Based on the theory, Ralph the Rat could learn to hit the bar because hitting the bar would release a yummy Purina Rat Chow pellet. Once Ralph met this standard, the experimenter could adjust the reinforcement schedule, gradually increasing the number of hits required to trigger the pellet reward. Raising the bar without raising the bar.

The experiment also tested our ability to shape the rat's behavior utilizing the remote. The rats had not been previously exposed to Skinner Box which required the researcher to hit the remote, triggering a reward when the rat demonstrated any behavior remotely close to the desired hitting the bar. Once that behavior was repeated, the reward was only given when the behavior was closer. Ralph was a superstar and didn't take long to get in shape.

Day 2 and I couldn't wait to train Ralph. I followed the procedures and Ralph calmly cooperated. He walked around the box, checking out his new digs. Ralph paused and pointed those pink eyes at the bar. He stood up and gently touched the bar with his front left paw. Click, clack, and he got a snack. Did not take long to understand that Ralph would have done better on his RATs than I did on my SATs. When I met with the admission counselor for Michigan, hello was not followed with "Welcome to the Michigan class of '76!", it was followed with "your SAT scores are a little low, but your dad went here, so we will make an exception."

When I told my dad, he chuckled and said they should have checked his first year law school grades before they admitted me.

Day 3, Ralph hit the bar and quickly discovered it wasn't by accident. Not sure whose behavior was being conditioned more, Ralph or mine. Think I even ditched going to the little house on the speed reading prairie to spend more time with Ralph. His performance was stellar, but I wanted more. Maybe it was compensating from going from a regular basketball starter since 7th grade to an infrequent substitute my senior year, or the admission counselor's comment, but I wanted Ralph to take home the Best Conditioned Rat trophy.

Day 4, we had reached 20 hits on the bar for one pellet. I did notice Ralph to be a bit more edgy and motivated. He even started biting the bar. When I finished the session and was sliding in his home cage, I spotted the Purina bag and it hit me. I forgot to feed Ralph on his regular schedule the day before.

Before I continue the story, I need to remind you that I was 18 years old, living vicariously through a rat's performance in a Skinner Box, loved my pets except the raccoons, still grieved my Rooster's mysterious disappearance, walked my dog every day and rescued critters with my net from my pool no matter how small. Just trying to mitigate the number and tone of the texts I am about to receive.

Decided I would cash in on my discovery and work on increasing Ralph's performance by purposely decreasing his daily food allotment. It worked with some minor modifications to the transfer from his home cage to the Skinner Box regiment. Ralph was so motivated that his calm demeanor transformed into jumping out and over his tiny house and quickly trying to bite the hand that wasn't feeding him. Invested in leather gloves and we were on our way to a record 100 hits for one pellet.

On day 6, my Teaching Assistant decided to visit the lab and check in on my progress. Ralph didn't disappoint, his pink eyes were laser focused, and he hit and bit the bar hard and fast, registering 120 hits before the click clack. The TA looked amazed and congratulated us for our hard work.

After storing my gloves, I left the lab almost tasting an A which would help the low grade I knew I was getting in Economics. Grabbed a bagel, returned to my dorm, and started working on my Philosophy class essay titled "Is Pleasure the Same thing as Happiness?" Three hours passed and unlike Ralph, my performance was less than stellar. I had to navigate a mountain of paper wads to answer the dorm room phone.

"Hello, this is your Psychology Lab Teaching Assistant. Have you been feeding your rat on the required schedule?" Silence. Today, it would fit the *awkward silence* Urban Dictionary definition. Before I could cobble together a response, my TA shouted, "I wanted to demonstrate your rat as a model for my afternoon class and when I took his cage out, he immediately stuck his head out and bit me. I am at the University Student Medical Clinic getting a tetanus shot." If I continued sharing this conversation, I would exceed my book swear word limit. My "A" became a "C" for failure to follow lab procedures, and whatever pleasure Ralph received from his pellets did not translate into my happiness.

We were both resilient. Ralph got back on a regular feeding schedule and, he went on to have a legendary career as a test subject for new cancer drugs. Researchers heard about his trauma in the Psych Lab and made sure he never got the placebo. I survived my cellar freshman G.P.A. and doubled-majored in Psychology and Education.

Ralph also taught me two legendary leadership lessons.

Promote, support, expand, and never cut after school extra-curricular sports and activities.

Remove Extra from Extra-Curricular

If I wasn't playing basketball after-school, I wouldn't have injured my leg. If I hadn't injured my leg, I wouldn't have gone to the hospital. If I hadn't gone to the hospital, I wouldn't have been bored. If I hadn't been bored, the nurse wouldn't have given me her psychology textbook. If I hadn't read the textbook, I wouldn't have taken my first psychology class. If I hadn't taken Psychology class, I wouldn't have met Ralph. If I hadn't met Ralph, I wouldn't have majored in Psychology, graduated, and become a teacher. (Author's note: This paragraph was inspired by the famous children's book "If You Give a Mouse a Cookie" by Laura Joffe Numeroff.)

Although Ralph's extraordinary performance in the Skinner Box supported behaviorist theory, it came with severe unintended consequences, frustration, violence, and blood. Reflecting, if I had kept Ralph on the "motivated" feeding schedule, his performance would have plummeted.

Leadership Lesson: before jumping into the newest, greatest performance pay plan for your organization, think about Ralph. He went from a kind, gentle white rat with a long tail and soft pink eyes to Ratzilla.

Don't starve the rat

Senior year and I had a practicum at the Perry Nursery School in Ann Arbor, Michigan. The Perry Nursery School (now called Foundations Preschool) started in 1934 and has had a long history of providing exceptional early learning experiences for young children. My role as a clinical student involved teaching, supervising, and observing three to five year olds learn and develop cognitively, socially, and emotionally.

The practicum turned into my first paying teaching job, 10 hours a week, and I usually worked the 3 p.m. to 6 p.m. shift. This job erased any doubt I had about choosing psychology and education as my majors. The teachers were amazing role models, and I was in awe of how they were able to energize, engage, and enlighten their young students every day.

The school was located in a renovated fraternity house which created a unique homelike learning environment. A favorite activity was taking the kids up to the fourth floor rumpus room, a retrofitted attic, which was padded from head to toe along with equipment which promoted active play.

The classrooms were designed around discovery and inquiry learning theory and had many different centers, including an animal corner. In October a student was moving, and he donated his hamster to the Perry family. The kids named her Heather and took turns with the care chores. Although I was tempted, I resisted creating a Psychology 101 lab, and Heather was allowed to just be a hamster, eating, drinking, and running on her rumpus room wheel.

When I came to work, I was quickly updated on school news which might impact my duties. No time for meetings, so the briefings were tweet-like. The big event one day was Heather's disappearance. She had escaped and was probably loving the multiple hiding places an old home provided. No panic, no stress, Perry life went on. I was told to be on the lookout for a little furry ball that moves on her own. A couple days went by and Heather was still a fugitive.

A week later, while walking through the classroom door, the head teacher mentioned the clock had stopped and if I got a chance, would I take a look at it. She obviously had not done a thorough check of my references. One quick call to Uncle Jim and she wouldn't have asked me to fix or build anything.

The children were outside, so I decided to try and break my perfect record by troubleshooting the clock problem. First step, took the clock off the wall which involved moving a large bookcase. Perry Nursery School had an innovative early childhood literacy program which included a large on-site loaner library located in the bookcase blocking access to the clock. Books relocated, bookcase moved one corner at a time, and clock mystery solved.

Actually, I scored a two-for, yet I wasn't high fiving. The reason the clock stopped is because Heather decided to wear down her teeth by chewing on the clock electric cord. An up-side to this story, we knew the exact time of death. I'm not the most sensitive guy in the world, but I did have enough sense not to point that fact out as the teacher made the announcement to the class.

We had learned about teacher intuition, recognizing teachable moments and optimizing the opportunity with rich and meaningful lessons. I was fortunate to observe master teachers transform this theory to practice. Heather's unfortunate accident was discussed with the kids and their many questions were answered with patience and care. A funeral service was held, including a small shoe box casket on which each student was allowed to draw a picture or write their name.

From tragedy to leadership lesson. Probably not my best bumper sticker. This is all I got at the moment. Maybe during the edit phase, I will do a deeper exploration into your cognitive cavern.

A missing hamster and a broken clock. On the surface, two separate, unrelated problems which logically require distinctly different possible solutions. After removing some logic blinders, the two problems become directly connected, with one going from problem to solution. Leaders often face the missing hamster / clock malfunction scenario. Leaders develop intuition and use their intuition to explore the possibility that two disconnected problems are connected. Peak performing leaders demonstrate courage to move the bookcase.

Heather's untimely demise taught me another powerful leadership lesson, yet I was too young and inexperienced for the lesson to stick. Forty years later and my grandson Timmy and a different rodent, a pack rat, legendized the lesson.

Six year old Timmy was visiting Grandpa and Grandma in Tucson for two weeks. On our walk through the wash, Timmy's curiosity led him to a nearly dead beaver tail cactus covered with a Chex Mix like combination of sticks, dried fruit, a red rubber ball, a maize and blue pom-pom, along with many unidentifiable objects. On close inspection, Timmy was able to I.D. one of these items; it was dried-up poo. My teacher gene kicked in, and we began our inquiry lesson by describing critical poo attributes and then matching to an animal which roamed this wash. Timmy put his deductive mind to work and determined that it was coyote poo.

Classroom bell hadn't rung yet. Next we started on figuring out what animal had created this stick and stuff masterpiece. Sometimes Grandpa has to sacrifice his own personal feelings for the sake of science.

This was the obvious work of my nemesis, the packrat. If Timmy wasn't with me, I would have gone off on a rant, describing pack rats as the raccoons of the desert, along with a few fourth grade descriptors about the $2000 car repair bill recently caused by those electric wire nibbling, air conditioning duct nest building critters.

To give some perspective on how adaptable packrats are, when I first moved to Tucson, I treated my packrat problem like I treated any rodent problem in Michigan: buy some D-Con and place the boxes around the back patio. After two days, checked my boxes and they were gone. Not just the blue pellets, the entire boxes. Another animal mystery to solve. If this book doesn't sell, might take Animal Mysteries and pitch it to a cable channel.

After moving every cabinet, I found the boxes. A packrat had carried them to add a second story to his nest.

Taking a true "every living creature is valuable approach," I tapped into Timmy's excitement and began elevating the packrat to king of the desert status. We took more walks, exploring every possible packrat nest we could find. I related my adventures to my graduate class and a student gifted the children's book, *Zachary Z. Packrat and His Amazing Collections* by Brooke Bressesen and Jenny Campbell. We read the book morning, noon, and night. Zachary Z. even had poo in his collection!

Two weeks were winding down and we took a break from Packrat 101 to swim. Timmy knew the pool cleaning routine, having helped earlier in the week. We picked up the pole, attached the skimming net, unlocked the gate, walked to the deep end. Timmy took one look and exclaimed, "Look grandpa, Zachary Z. went swimming before us and he is doing the backstroke!"

Packrats have many strengths: nest building, drought resistance, poo artistry. But swimming, front, side, or back stroke is not on this list.

Instantly forgot I was Grandpa who had spent two weeks building packrat memories. Pool Boy Nic instincts kicked in, and I took the pole, skimmed the exalted yet dead rodent into the net, and catapulted him into my neighbor's yard.

Timmy immediately started with questions which I attempted to answer. What happened? He drowned. How did he drown? He got water in his lungs. How and why didn't we call 911? You stumped me at how. What side of the pool did he try to get out of? The stairs. Since he couldn't web surf and fact check my answers, like my grad students, I started making stuff up. Where is his mom? In the nest we found down in the wash.

After at least 20 more questions, I did what I should have done when my daughter's guinea pig died in 1992: follow my Perry Nursery School mentors and have a proper funeral service. Pet guinea pig Spot died when I was home alone, and I decided to save her the trauma by quickly digging a hole next to the wash. Immediate tears followed by "Why did you bury him before I got home?" admonishment triggered a trip to the back yard. Fortunately the makeshift grave was marked by fresh shovel half-moons.

We retrieved Zachary Z., apologizing to my neighbor as he stood watering the grass and shaking his head. Timmy got a box and we had a memorial, a proper burial, and laid him to rest with a gravestone next to Spot's mausoleum.

Lead with empathy

Leadership lessons are obvious, and you are wondering why it took so long for me to get it. Beginning to agree with my University of Michigan admission counselor? Leaders must combine patience with the ability to answer hard questions, and understand that sincere answers lead to awareness which builds trust.

Most importantly, next time a rodent dies, put your smart phone down, look your colleagues in the eye, and say some nice words at the funeral.

Chapter 3 Engagers

- What is the RAT?

- How do you recognize and reward performance? Does it work? How do you know?

- What does energize, engage, and enlighten look like in your organization?

- Create a Legendary Leadership Lesson bumper sticker capturing this chapter.

Chapter Four

Control Your Bullwinkle

Chapter Four

Control Your Bullwinkle

Wonder how Freud would interpret a recurring dream where I am driving to Phoenix and when I get to the Chandler exit, I forget how to drive. I thought this was one of those common dreams like flying or falling into a toilet. After polling audiences attending my presentations and workshops over the last two years, I am stressed to discover it is not close to common. Mine and mine alone, and it is getting worse. A recent version of the dream: froze at exit 160, hands gripping the wheel at 10 and 2, look down and I am naked.

If I get therapy, might as well bring up the other recurring dream. I have had this one since 1962, when I first watched the Macy's Thanksgiving Day Parade. A week later, I began dreaming that I was a rope bearer, helping control and steer my favorite giant balloon, Bullwinkle the Moose. Often, the dream involves (yes, still having it) Bullwinkle being blown away, lifting me off the ground and taking me with him. Other times, I muscle Bullwinkle away from the hundred other rope holders, and we go and find a theater stage. The dream really goes deep when the Bullwinkle balloon gets on stage, starts talking, and says "Hey Rocky, wanna see me pull a rabbit out of my hat?"

While I wait for book royalties to fund my psychoanalysis, (might be a long wait with a chapter titled "Control Your Bullwinkle"), I should prep with some research.

According to Wikipedia, The Bullwinkle the Moose balloon first appeared in 1961 and has had a rocky history. In 1982, Bullwinkle sprung a leak in his nose and then in 1983, his handlers almost lived my nightmare when the heavy winds pushed his head and legs together.

Bullwinkle the Moose took out a lamppost in 1997, and he didn't make the parade in 2000, deflating in the prep barn.

Could my dreams be foreshadowing the future? Naw, if that were true, I would have been arrested for indecent exposure last week when I drove to Phoenix. I also would have flunked out of Michigan. For four years, OK—five years—I often woke up in a sweat from the "I can't find my college classes" dream. I imagine some of my professors (Economics 90) wished that dream was a reality.

I am sure when I start therapy, we will do word association. Pretending to be the therapist (I did have one psychopathology class), we will think about the three key dream words: Thanksgiving, Parade, and Balloons. Let's start with THANKSGIVING. Give me the first word that comes to your mind. MASSAGE

Not what you are thinking, and not what Freud would be thinking if he was my therapist? Second Thanksgiving as a married couple, living in an apartment in Las Vegas, and my recently married brother and his wife came to visit. We convinced our wives that there were so many buffets on the Strip, that we could forgo the traditional turkey with all the fixings dinner. At about 1 p.m., the wives realize that we had replaced the Thanksgiving buffet table with the blackjack table. 2 p.m., my brother and I were at the local supermarket, scrambling to find a small turkey. We found a turkey, the last one, and it was far from small. I dove into the freezer, my brother held my legs, and we pulled out what appeared to be a big chunk of the iceberg that took down the Titanic. Figured this bird had been at the freezer bottom since Labor Day. Only good news, we could use the freezer burn to make frozen margaritas.

Having minimal experience thawing a turkey, we decided to put it in the sink and run water over it. In reality we had NO experience thawing turkeys. "Minimal" has professorial "they are not complete idiots" ring to it. Remember this is 1979 B.S. and our wives were out shopping for fixings. We were experiencing some urgency, urgency to save a family tradition and urgency to recover from splitting sevens with the dealer showing a six. We hit and got another seven. Split that hand. Dealer gave us a ten on all three sevens. We are sitting pretty on three seventeens. The dealer had a two of spades as a down card, and hits a King of Hearts.

Now the turkey's was in the sink, water running. The only thing left was to psswissh some beers and watch football. Figured the turkey would be thawed by half-time, girls would stuff it, throw it in the oven and admire the table we set with plastic silverware and a beautiful centerpiece. We spared no expense. Flat until you release the little metal hook, then viola, it sprang into a giant paper cornucopia. We fashioned an accompanying "we're sorry" hand-made card and taped it to the door. Literally hand-made: traced our hands and drew an eye and a mouth, Abracadabra, a turkey appeared. Finally, that art project I got a "C" on in 3rd grade was paying off.

The wives' return did not go as predicted. Instead of the "what a beautiful table, mom had that same centerpiece when we were young" smile and "a turkey card you made yourself" aww, we got the "are you two guys crazy?" look. I could have used the "what were you guys thinking?" look, but that already was taken by another chapter.

After an hour under the faucet, the turkey was still far from oven ready. Didn't help that we left all the frozen giblets inside, insulating and further slowing down the thaw. We needed a new strategy quick to thaw the turkey and the glare.

Mentally picture two grown men (wives would argue that adjective) trying to watch football and drink beer while vigorously massaging with both hands a large turkey as water is splashed from the faucet above. Ok, stop, don't want you to experience a reoccurring nightmare. Trying to capitalize on my own dreams and do not need you writing a similar book and competing with my Amazon key word search.

If I thought our technique would have a remote chance of being replicated, I would contact *foodsafety.gov* and suggest they update their Turkey Thawing Chart to include: Turkey Size: 20-24 lbs. In Refrigerator: 5-6 days: Under Cold Water: 10-12 hours. Massaged by two thoughtless guys: 3-4 hours. Survey says, save my keystrokes.

If I was the therapist with me on the couch, at this moment, I would excuse myself, stick my head in the outer office, and ask the administrative assistant if another patient was waiting so I wouldn't have to suffer through another word association story. If it wasn't my lucky day, I would follow-up with, "And what did we learn from this experience?"

Legendary leadership lesson: don't mess with tradition, or you will be massaging a mess. Leaders will find it difficult to change the future if they don't know and honor the past.

Honor the past, celebrate the present, challenge the future

Therapist sighs, followed by "next word, PARADE... what is the first word that comes to your mind? Therapist cringes when the word PAIN quickly comes across my lips. Amazing, therapist and reader thinking exactly the same word.

In my small town, a big tradition growing up was participating in the Memorial Day Parade. My dad would saddle up our three donkeys, Jack, Jenny, and their one year old son Burrs (born in a burr bush), tie some U.S. flags on the reins, and take the "Santa, his sleigh and twelve tiny reindeer" parade position. Unlike Santa, riding a donkey was not climatic, nor were spectators putting their children on their shoulders for the best view. It was a position of convenience. Dad had bridle in one hand and clean up shovel in the other.

Jack and Jenny were experienced parade strutters. More like they had learned that once a year they would have to tolerate someone on their back, and red, white, and blue streamers coming out of their ears. This was my and Burrs' first parade. Started out great. Burrs was patient as I struggled with climbing in the saddle. After the tenth try, we began, and made the turn down Main Street from the school parking lot staging area. About 100 yards down the parade route, Burrs started to send me some signals that he wasn't crazy about the crowd, the band, the fine looking thoroughbred horses with blue 4-H ribbons hanging from their hand tooled saddles leading the parade, and me on his back. Couple hind leg kicks with corresponding toots, and Burrs turned his head to the left, looked me in the eye, and saw me laughing (something about toots, can't control myself. Still crack up every time I watch *Blazing Saddles*). Burrs didn't appreciate my lack of empathy for his humiliating circumstance, and turns to the right and bites my leg. I yelled, kicked him in the side, he bit me again and I tooted. Jack and Jenny paused, brayed a laugh, and nodded their proud approval to their son standing up for himself.

Still have the scar, and every time I see it reminds me: don't make a parade the first time you jump on a donkey. Another legendary leadership lesson. As I grew up, I learned to appreciate Burrs for his strengths: eating pears bareback and tooting without ridicule.

Lead with your gifts

Therapist: Are you done with your asinine story? Here's your next word: BALLOON. If you say TOOT, I am walking out and you can do your own therapy. Me: a chuckle followed by the word MEETING.

Here is a take on an overused idiom: if I had a dollar for every hour I spent in a meeting, I would be able to hold my pinky to the side of my mouth and quote Austin Powers, "One million dollars." Reality check. If I had a dollar for every hour I spent in an effective, productive meeting where participants listened and respected each other, I would have a lot less money yet be a lot richer.

People should not leave their egos at the door before they enter a meeting. Egos bring life, creativity, different perspectives, and out of the

Skinner Box, thinking to problem solving and strategic planning.

There is a delicate dynamic which occurs in meetings between egos stimulating imagination and inspiration, and egos which deaden communication and collaboration.

Egos are like Thanksgiving parade balloons: colorful, unique, shapeless without lighter-than-air gas, and challenging to control even on a sunny day. If we all enter a meeting room with our balloons filled to capacity, prepared for a long parade, odds are high that Mickey, Snoopy, the Trolls, Felix, and Trixie will start bumping into each other, and the guide ropes will get tangled.

When this happens in meetings, our favorite balloon characters' names and personalities Here are a few not so favorite meeting balloons.

Topper: Before a meeting participant can even finish their idea, Topper interrupts and gives what they believe is a bigger, better version of the same idea. Topper's balloon handlers release the slack, making Topper go higher than every other team member's balloon.

Reducer: After you have shared your idea, Reducer immediately shares reasons why your idea will not work. Reducer attempts to poke holes and shrink your balloon with "too expensive," "we've tried it before," and "that's a crazy idea" statements.

Revenger: As their balloon hisses, Revenger waits until Reducer shares a brilliant idea, and Revenger takes a pin and returns the favor with a "the last superintendent got fired for that initiative" hisser.

Resenter: Resenter has been topped, reduced, and revenged to the point that Resenter breaks through the orange barrier and leaves the parade route.

Parades with "out of control" balloons are no fun and a little scary. No one wants to be standing under the street lamp that Bullwinkle takes out. Meetings with toppers, reducers and revengers are also no fun and real scary. The purpose of meetings is to tap into the "two heads are better than one" synergy. If heads are being topped, reduced, and revenged, you mentally leave the meeting and resentment is the street of no return.

Walla Walla Washington, my Bullwinkle dream makes sense! A leadership lesson in facilitating dynamic and productive meetings is as clear as his antlers are wide.

Let some air out of your ego balloon before you enter the meeting room and get a strong hold on the guide ropes. Don't be a topper, reducer, revenger, or resenter. Be a listener, accepter, thinker, and a piggy backer. Control your Bullwinkle, and the parade will be a success in spite of wind, rain, or donkey bites.

Ideas — listen, accept, and piggy back

Chapter 4 Engagers

- What does B.S. stand for in 1979 B.S.?

- Describe your first donkey ride in a leadership parade.

- What is the deeper meaning of Walla Walla, Washington?

- What are your strategies for dealing with toppers, reducers, and revengers?

Chapter Five
Free for All

Chapter Five

Free for All

Time to go rogue, break all the literary rules, and finally speak my mind. Unlike the first four chapters where I meticulously followed the story line outlines, carefully chose my words, and strictly mirrored leadership book formulas, this chapter will be random, reeling, and yes, legendary.

Life jacket

Growing up on a ski lake provided great motivation for learning to swim. Sooner you could swim, sooner you could ski. Swimming lessons didn't happen at the YMCA. Our swimming lessons involved wearing an orange life jacket, bobbing on our own for a full summer and then graduating by climbing up the high dive ladder, parents taking our jacket off, throwing the jacket in the water which was followed by us jumping off and swimming out to the raft. This system worked for first three kids and dad had the Super 8 movies to prove it.

Then it is Lefty's summer. If they made right-handed life jackets, my mom would have purchased one. Red rubber boots and life jackets last forever, so I was fitted with a jacket that had my older brothers' names crossed out and my name written in white water resistant paint, the same paint we used one summer to write our names on turtles we caught. Each summer we would have contests. Who could continuously ski around the lake the longest? Who could jump off the high dive, into the muck, and stay down the longest, and come up with the longest mud stain on their leg? Who could re-catch a turtle with your name painted on its back?

Throughout the book, you have noticed that I continually use the "age card" to explain and excuse my behavior. Since I have no other line of defense, painting turtles with oil based paint was done when I was five.

Aggravating your anger further, the paint probably had lead in it.

If you are going to blast me with another email, add in the fact that at the same age, I ran through the DDT fog when my dad's friend would come over to spray for mosquitoes. As you practice the 24 hour rule, you might recall that one spring break, my brother and I cleaned out the donkey barn and created the world's largest compost pile which organically fertilized our neighbors' gardens for years. Still sending the email with a cc to the Environmental Protection Agency? Understandable, but it was worth a shot.

Midway through the freestyle stroke induction summer, mom noticed that I was doing more bobbing than swimming. I was "encouraged" to use my arms (especially my right one) and legs more. In September, my parents decided to postpone my graduation trip up the high dive and gave me another summer with my orange jacket mentor.

No big deal at the time. As I got older, the "Nic just needs more time" pattern started to get old. Needs more time putting on his boots and leggings, needs more time practicing to drive, needs more time going to the dermatologist and the orthodontist, needs more time at the little house on the reading prairie, and needs more time (10 years) to complete his doctorate.

Need more time to analyze that revelation and the connection to leadership? See how it feels?

Spring, excited to help put the dock in, not excited about pulling that orange vest out from being stored under one of the dock support poles the entire winter. Paint lived up to its additives, and name was still bright and obvious. It was my younger brother's learn to swim year, he got a new jacket.

My swim performance evaluation during Fourth of July week, not stellar. Coaching reinforcements brought in, including neighbor's Irish setter who could swim the length of the lake and often did while chasing skiers. Even the muskrat who lived in the lily pads in front of Jake's who took a daily early morning swim past the dock was touted as a great role model.

Labor Day, and the parents took a risk announcing my graduation with minor accommodations. The ceremonial life jacket tossing and subsequent jumping in would be done from the dock instead of the high dive. Reflecting, it made some sense. Dad's lifesaver leap from the dock would be much less painful from 6 inches versus 10 feet.

Mom's toss went about five feet in the air and landed between dock and raft. Sure, that was calculated to give me a panic option. Before the countdown for my jump, the entire family watched as the orange life jacket, white letters up, hit the water and proceeded to immediately sink to the bottom of the lake. Sank so fast and hard, it would have won the muck contest. Before the count started, I jumped in, swam like Spitz, went under, retrieved the orange devil, touched the raft, and swam back. I was smiling; mom's mouth was in the same position it was in that winter night when I crawled down the new, too short fire escape ladder.

In the '60s, life jackets were made of kapok, a waxy vegetable fiber sealed in plastic. Have you seen a kapok life jacket lately at the local pool? Have you run through DDT fog in the last 40 years? The answer to these questions is a big NO because they were both determined to be extremely hazardous to your health.

DDT was found to cause cancer, and kapok life jackets were found to become soggy anchors when the plastic covering was punctured. Punctured, like what might happen when an old orange life jacket is stored under dock poles with large pointed spiral ends needed to auger the poles into the mud.

Good news: I went swimming the next year when the ice broke and started learning to ski right after the Memorial Day parade. Took a little more time to master the "let the boat pull you up" and made my first lake circle without falling on the Fourth of July.

Couple of swim away conversations. Don't run through DDT and you can't judge a life jacket by the bright orange cover.

Don't rely on your life jacket to keep you afloat

Fully Engaged or Stand Arounds

October, and I am running around updating my passport. Excited and a bit anxious about an upcoming consulting engagement with Mazapan, a PK-12 school in La Ceiba, Honduras. Hadn't traveled outside the country for years. Knowing my past history with unfamiliar places, procedures and routines, your head is nodding approval for my concern. I was particularly cautious about getting the recommended immunizations.

Completed my trip, and realized I had over stressed. Smooth flights. Incredible students, incredible teachers, incredible leaders, incredible hospitality, and returned healthier than I left—mentally and physically. Mazapan had an engaging culture rarely observed in schools. A culture built by design and implemented with fidelity by Mazapan teachers, staff, principals, superintendents, and governing board members. Leadership lesson: leadership doesn't happen unless engagement occurs.

November, fall cleanup time in Michigan, and I decided last minute to fly in and take a long weekend to help my brothers with some projects. No shots, no bag (just carry on), and got the Tucson airport routine down like a seasoned second grader lining up for library time. So confident, I got to the airport at 8:02 a.m. and my flight left at 10:00 a.m.

As I sauntered through the security screening, face beaming, with "I recently traveled to Honduras" confidence, I noticed the x-ray belt had stopped at the exact moment my carry-on bag was up for inspection. My mind and body went into code blue alert when a TSA agent removed my carry-on and asked me to step to that small area no traveler wants to visit.

The agent began a thorough bag search, something I had obviously not done in years. Good thing TSA requires gloves and current shot records for agents. There was a frown on the agent's face, and a cringe on my entire body, as a copper colored CO_2 cartridge was pulled from my bag.

In my presentations, I sometimes end with a shot from my confetti cannon, powered by a small CO_2 cartridge, the same cartridge which powers pellet guns. I have had sense enough to never travel with the cannon yet didn't have sense enough to properly dispose of the spent cartridge after a recent keynote.

I admire TSA for the job they are doing, keeping air travel safe which includes a next level review for my infraction. Didn't think I needed a shower or deodorant for my Michigan trip. Traveling alone, and if I start cleaning up to hang out with my brothers, the end of the world must be near. Wished I had at least put that Old Spice (it's making a comeback) stick up my shirt, and made a couple of swipes.

Web search "Airport Travel Big Time No-Nos" and a picture of me, forehead sweat beads glistening, standing in front of a TSA Agent continuing to search my black carry-on, pops up in the number one position.

Stuffed frogs and rubber ducks are additional props for some presentations. Had a few in my carry-on bag which the agent found. Maybe attempting to break my perspiration and tension, the agent commented, "My grandkids collect these ducks." I quickly respond, "Great, I have grandkids, and they like them too. Please, take some for your grandkids. Pick the ones you think they would like and take some frogs. I just ordered a case of each." Nervous TMI rambling interrupted by agent stating, "No, that would be a bribe, and it is strictly prohibited."

Shaken and stirred, me and my frogs and ducks were eventually released with the familiar, "Take more time packing and checking your carry-on, sir." The agent did add "sir" which was different from the end words my parents and former bosses would use.

The flight to Michigan was uneventful except for my constant self-talk apologies. Although mom made progress in her goal to raise a right handed, ready for the world son, she unfortunately ran out of time.

My brother's project the day before I returned home involved helping him move dead trees, making room for future blueberry bush planting. Beyond a photo op on the John Deere front loader, engagement—operating the chain saw and chain wrapping the logs—was minimal.

TSA and brother's motto: safety first. Like the airport screening experience, I stood around and watched professionals work.

Returned home, and the first suggestion I received was to take off my three day old shirt. During the summer at the lake, showers were optional. In my case, non-existent. An occasional soaping down after muck jumping seemed to work. 63 years old, and I applied the 10 year old, July, body hygiene rules.

Before throwing the crunchy shirt into the washer, my wife noticed something unusual on my back. On closer examination using rat bite proof gloves, tweezers, a Saturn Rings telescope, and a DDT spill hazmat suit, her diagnosis: a tick found its way through airport security and through my first couple of epidermal layers. Attempts to burn the sucker with a match generated big screams and little success.

Thought standing face to face with TSA Agent waiting for a fly or no fly verdict was embarrassing. Have new top 10 most embarrassing moment. Laying on my side at Urgent Care, knowing there were actual sick people in the waiting room, and the doctor was using her scalpel to dig out the tiny critter. The doctor's bedside manner was superb: "Good that you came in. Arizona doesn't have Lyme disease, but it is rampant in the woods in Michigan. There, got the bugger. Not too engorged with blood, so it probably hasn't been on your back more than 48 hours. We need to do a preventive Lyme disease treatment, and I will be right back and get you a prescription."

As I was putting on my clean shirt and hoping I could navigate back to the reception area, a couple of ideas swirled around my humiliation. Eight to ten years of medical school and my doctor referred to the tick as a "bugger." I know how hard it was for her not to use the scientific name, Ixodes Scapularis, or at least reference it as a parasite who lives off the blood of a host. She was the smartest person in the room yet chose not to flaunt it.

Fully engorge on that legendary leadership lesson.

Ticks love leaders who stand around

48 hours, proof positive my stowaway jumped on board when I was passively helping my brother move logs. Leadership lesson: leaders who stand around and watch get ticks.

Tiny Crystal Salt and Pepper Shakers

Took a recent spring cleanup, Tucson to Michigan trip. Arrived two hours early, checked my bag at the curb, no carry-on, no ducks, frogs or ticks, had digital boarding passes, and gate change in Dallas was located in the same terminal. By the time the pilot announced we were 30,000 feet over New Mexico, coffee and a Lotus Biscoff had been served with a smile. Small print on the small package said "Europe's Favorite Cookie with Coffee." Thought, wow, moving on up. Usually only get pretzels.

Put the tray down, squeezed arm and legs together to fully comply with center seat personal space protocols, and started savoring my first cookie. Then it happened. Remember the bright light aura surrounding Snow White as the "It's A Small World" ride boats came to the end? It was happening again. I noticed the airline flight attendant coming down the aisle had a similar glow. She stopped at my aisle, turned to me, and said, "Due to a booking problem, we are going to upgrade you to First Class for your connection between Dallas and Grand Rapids." Would have unbuckled and hugged, but the fastened seat belt light was on and a rule violation would have resulted in detention (seat in back by toilet) and my upgrade being given to Kevin.

I entered Grand Rapids flight, even before families with children. Wanted to fit in. I observed frequent first classers and tried to emulate the "attitude." My first dilemma was that the flight attendant was already serving drinks and I couldn't find the tray. Told myself, act cool or you will never be upgraded again. My drink is delivered expertly wrapped in a cloth napkin. Held it and drank it like I was at a party- - head down, no eye contact. First first class crisis averted. I wasn't asked to move to seat 50 C.

I started to get comfortable, and sink into the rich Corinthian leather when the attendant startled me by laying a white cloth across my lap and asking what I wanted to order for lunch. Order for lunch! Panic!

I couldn't be seen holding a lunch tray and eating like a donkey at a trough. Then the passenger next to me lifted the cover to the arm rest and pulled out a folding tray. Lifetime ban averted.

Similar to putting together furniture or my grandkid's new toy, I got excited with the initial success and didn't read the instructions to the end. As the deadline approached, I scrambled to retrieve and unfold the tray. The end near my left hand had a thin shape like a paddle. Couldn't find the slot to push into it because there wasn't one. After 10 tries, observed the passenger in 3 D who gently laid the end of the folding tray on the armrest top.

Cloth napkin was wrinkled and full of Biscoff crumbs from a half-eaten cookie stored in my front pocket. The attendant pretended not to notice and placed the magnificent lunch before me. Not only another Halo, this time there was ahhhhh music. Silverware (real—no sporks), neatly draped with lily white cloth napkins, three square porcelain dishes matched to the size of each course. Fresh salad with vine ripe cherry tomatoes, cut in half to prevent me from squirting tomato juice into the cockpit. A corned beef sandwich on swirled rye bread with aged cheddar cheese. Assorted fresh raw vegetables arranged in lines. Chocolate cake with double chocolate frosting, topped with a strawberry. Butter shaped like a jetliner, and tiny crystal salt and pepper shakers.

If passengers and crew hadn't already gotten drift that I was a First Class first timer, taking my phone out to snap a *lunchie* and asking "what is this for?" when the attendant delivered the hot towel, sealed my fate.

May have noticed this last story lacks conflict, questionable decision making, parent involvement, ride malfunctions, or donkeys farting. Where's the Legendary Leadership Lesson context?

My most relaxed, happiest experience generated the most painful, powerful leadership lesson.

Every student deserves a personalized, first class educational experience, complete with fine linen and tiny crystal salt and pepper shakers. The ultimate leadership challenge is to make this dream come true. Have the courage to be a legendary leader and do the right thing, the right way for the right reasons, guaranteeing that all students fly first class every day.

Chapter 5 Engagers

- What is the 24 hour rule and why is it critical for leaders to follow?

- Describe an organizational "DDT" fog that you have avoided.

- Who is Kevin and why would he be the first one upgraded?

- How do you prevent office addiction and the associated standing around symptoms?

- What are you doing tomorrow to upgrade your students from Coach to First Class?

All students should fly First Class